"For the Jews there was light and joy, gladness and honor."

(Megillas Esther 8:16)

The Shushan

The Story of Purim Based on the Midrash

Chronicle

By Yaffa Leba Gottlieb
Illustrated by Aidel Backman

*This book is dedicated in memory of
Alta Mina bas Yisocher Shlomo, a"h
and with gratitude to my husband and teacher,
Yaakov Eliezer Gottlieb*

The Shushan Chronicle is based on Midrashim.

THE SHUSHAN CHRONICLE

FIRST EDITION
First Impression — MARCH 1991

Published by HaChai Publishing

Copyright © 1991 by HaChai Publishing
ALL RIGHTS RESERVED

This book, or parts thereof, may not be reproduced, stored, or copied in any form without written permission from the copyright holder, except by a reviewer who wishes to quote brief passages in connection with a review written for inclusion in magazines or newspapers.

THE RIGHTS OF THE COPYRIGHT HOLDER
WILL BE STRICTLY ENFORCED.

ISBN 0—922613—39—7 (Casebound Edition)
ISBN 0—922613—40—0 (Softcover Edition)
ISBN 0—922613—41—9 (Cassette Tape)

Distributed by: HaChai Distributions
705 Foster Avenue ● Brooklyn, New York 11230
(718) 692-3900

Printed in Hong Kong

The Shushan Chronicle

The Throne

Achashveirosh, the mighty king of Persia, stood in the grand throne room of his awesome Shushan palace — suffering! He ruled 127 provinces, yet he suffered. Every prince from Hodu to Kush sent him gifts and gold, and still he suffered. His wife Vashti was the most famous and beautiful queen of all the lands — yet he suffered! Achashveirosh suffered because . . . he could not sit on his throne!

And what an amazing throne it was! Shimmering with gold, gleaming with ivory, sparkling with jewels — diamonds, rubies, sapphires, like stars in the heavens. Wonderful animals carved of pure gold stood on the seven steps that led up to the throne — lions, eagles, dove, bull, wolf, and peacock! How Achashveirosh longed to climb, step by step, to the very top.

"Oh, please, Your Royal Majesty! Do not sit there!" cautioned the Sunday advisor, bowing so low that his pointed hat tickled his toes. "If His Royal Highness were to sit on this throne —"

"His Royal Highness's royal leg could get bashed in!" The Monday advisor got right to the point.

"That's what happened to Nevuchadnetzar, the great king of Babylon!" exclaimed Tuesday's advisor. "After he conquered Jerusalem, after he burned the Holy Temple, after he captured the Jews and marched them in chains to Babylon — well, then, he marched this throne back to Babylon too. *This* throne! The famous throne of Solomon, king of the Jews! But the second that Nevuchadnetzar's toe touched the first step —"

"The golden lion swiped him, and Nevuchadnetzar limped for the rest of his life!" the Wednesday advisor finished. "And the same thing happened to Shaistak, the Lame Pharaoh of Egypt!"

"Yet, my honored father Coresh sat on this throne!" Achashveirosh protested.

"Yes, he did, but for a particular reason," the Thursday advisor reminded. "Your honored father Coresh had promised to rebuild the Jewish Temple."

"But *you* don't want to do that, Your Majesty!" Haman, the Saturday advisor, rushed in before his turn. "Your Majesty! You so wisely ordered the Jews to *stop* building their Temple — for the safety of Persia! Remember the warning my loyal sons gave you: Behind those Temple walls, the Jews are planning to rebel!"

Rebel? Achashveirosh turned pale. The Jews *seemed* to be loyal citizens! Could it really be that they were secretly plotting to take over the country? Indeed, even the stars in the heavens seemed to say so! For the royal stargazers were predicting that the next king of Persia would be — a Jew!

A Jew? A Jew sit on *his* throne? No! Never! Achashveirosh would get rid of the Jews! Eliminate! Obliterate! Exterminate every one!

But how?

The Plan

"Well!" thought Achashveirosh when he was alone that night. "What can I do about these Jews? I am a kind and benevolent king! A just and humanitarian king! A murderous act would damage my reputation, impair my credibility, and who knows? People might not even like me anymore! Besides, the Jewish G-d often saves His Jews. Sooner or later He punishes their enemies with horrifying miracles!

"But would He be able to do that now?"

The king began to pace. "Hmmmm, let's see. The Jewish prophets said that the Jews would be exiled from the Land of Israel for seventy years. Well, how many has it been so far? Since Nevuchadnetzar left to conquer Jerusalem — hmmm! It's already *been* seventy years! Seventy years, and their G-d hasn't saved them. Well, if He hasn't saved them by now, He never will!"

He brightened. "Now, *that's* worth celebrating! I should have a party!

"And I'll invite the Jews to celebrate too. I'll make sure that they have such a good time, with such delicious food, that they'll forget about their G-d — and they'll break *all* His Jewish laws! Then He will *certainly* never help them!

"Yes!" murmured the king. "A party!"

The Feast

"Over here, boy! A drink!"

"Oh! I-I can't! I just can't!" Fariboblil, the youngest cup-fetcher of the Royal Shushan Kitchen, gasped as he staggered up the steep stone steps of the wine cellar. "Oh! The governor of Moav is calling me again, asking for his forty-seventh cup of wine! My poor legs! For 180 days I've had to run up and down, up and down these steps. Thousands of governors and noblemen from all the 127 provinces — all feasting, and all drinking! I can't even turn around without someone shouting —"

"More wine, boy!"

"But I can't just pour wine for them! The king wants everyone to have a different pure gold goblet for every drink — to take home as a souvenir!"

"Drink up — keep the cup!" roared the governor of Moav. "Over here, boy!"

So poor Fariboblil made his way through the crowded gardens. His mouth watered at the exotic foods that had been prepared by cooks from all over the world, but he had to hold onto his heavy tray with both hands and could not even sneak a taste. Above him, gigantic blue, green, and white silken canopies hung on silver rods from marble poles to protect the guests from the sun.

"A feast fit for a king!" marveled a guest.

"*And* a queen!" added another. "Queen Vashti has insisted on equally fine dining for the ladies!"

"Am I glad this is the last day!" gasped Fariboblil. "I can't carry another cup!"

"But didn't you hear?" asked Zlipblip, the vegetable peeler. "*This* banquet was just for practice! Now Achashveirosh wants the city of Shushan, and the Jews as well, to feast for seven days more!"

Ben Begged, a tailor who lived in the Jewish quarter of Shushan, was amazed to see the king's soldiers standing at his door.

"His Majesty invites you to his royal banquet!" the chief guard proclaimed.

"But how can we go?" Ben Begged whispered to his wife. "Didn't Mordechai warn us not to feast with kings so long as our Holy Temple is in ruins?"

"B-but how can we *not* go?" whispered his wife. "They look like they expect us to come and enjoy the royal feast."

And how delightful it was!

"What a garden the king has!" exclaimed Ben Begged. "Such rainbows of flowers! Fragrant perfumes — mm! And such food! Ah — like Gan Eden! Surely *some* of it must be kosher . . . Oh! Why, thank you!"

A waiter holding a dazzling bowl offered Ben Begged a luscious Aramean pear. Ben Begged held the heavy fruit in his hand, but his eyes were drawn to the fruit bowl — that golden bowl . . .

Gold! As Ben Begged gazed at its brilliance, he nearly dropped his pear. Only one kind of gold in the world was so fine and pure — the gold used to make the vessels of the Holy Temple!

Was Achashveirosh using the holy vessels as fruit bowls? How could it be?

Ben Begged shivered. Once, King Balshatzar of Babylon had tried to serve strawberries from the holy vessels — and he had died that very night! And here were Achashveirosh and Vashti, who had been ladling stew from the vessels for months now.

And what were they wearing? The sacred robes of the *Kohen Gadol*? Yes! Ben Begged nearly fainted. They were wearing the holy robes as party gowns — yet nothing had happened to them!

Ben Begged leaned against a marble pillar and seized a silk napkin to wipe his brow. Didn't G-d care anymore? Had G-d forgotten His people? Perhaps things were different now that the Jews were living in Shushan, so far away from the Holy Land. There, G-d had expected every Jew to learn Torah and keep mitzvos. But maybe G-d didn't care what they did in Shushan!

Ben Begged grew sick. He reached for a pastry and sipped some wine, hoping to feel better.

The king watched. Achashveirosh was delighted to see that his plan had worked. Look at the Jews! They were eating! They were drinking! They were forgetting about their G-d and His special laws!

On the seventh day of the feast, however, not one Jew came. This day happened to be both Shabbos and Yom Kippur. Even the most party-loving Jew would not break the laws of those holy days to join a feast, even the feast of a king.

Achashveirosh sighed. Still, he had made the Jews break their laws for six days out of seven. Perhaps that was enough. Now the king could join his guests and celebrate too! Soon Achashveirosh's face flushed pink as raspberries, and his heart grew merry.

The Queen

With a foggy smile, Achashveirosh stretched and leaned back contentedly in his chair. "Ah! What good wine! Wonderful wine! A wonderful kingdom, wonderful guests — burp! — wonderful friends, and a wonderful wife! Beautiful queen, Vashti! What a queen!"

"Ah, yes!" exclaimed Maradav, a courtier, as he thumped his empty cup on the table. "If you want to see beautiful women, look at Persian women! The most beautiful in the world!"

"Only if you're blind," retorted Ierkirk, an officer of Media. "Median women — *they* have beauty!"

"Listen to me, my dear friends!" cried Achashveirosh. "Certainly all women are beautiful! But the most beautiful one of all is from Babylon — my queen, Vashti!"

"Vashti!" Ierkirk was drunk enough to dare to argue with the king. "Any woman would be beautiful dressed as a queen!"

"Let Vashti come in, and you shall see how beautiful she is!" thundered Achashveirosh. "Here, boy," he called to Fariboblil. "Go to Vashti and have her come here at once!"

"Me? Tell the queen?"

So flabbergasted was Fariboblil that he nearly tripped over a Jewish slave girl who was scrubbing the queen's courtyard floor. Fariboblil turned his face away, ashamed. Vashti was even more cruel than her grandfather Nevuchadnetzar, the wicked Babylonian king. She forced her Jewish slave girls to work without rest.

Fariboblil reached the door of Vashti's chamber and delivered his message to the lady-in-waiting. Soon everyone heard the reply.

"*Drunken fool!*"

The silken canopies trembled as Vashti shrieked.

"That miserable tyrant, the king, is not fit to clean my father's stables! *I*, a princess of Babylon, show my beauty before his guests? I will *not* come!"

"*Not come?*" Achashveirosh repeated when he heard the reply, and turned beet red. "Have my top ministers *command* her to come!"

"Never!" Vashti snarled when the message came.

"Now!" the ministers insisted. "Or the king could order your death."

So Vashti relented. She smoothed her hair, adjusted her crown, glanced once again in the mirror . . .

And nearly fainted. A horrid, bumpy rash had spread over her body. And on her lower back — a lump! As if she were growing a tail!

"I-I-I can't come," she whispered.

And Achashveirosh roared. In front of everyone, the queen dared to disobey the king? By the law of Persia, she deserved to die! But how could he kill his lovely Vashti? Achashveirosh was completely befuddled, and he bellowed for advice. But what could his counselors say? Can you tell a king to kill his wife?

"Ahem!" Haman, the Saturday advisor, was the only one willing to speak.

All was clear to Haman. Was Vashti guilty? Of course she was. Vashti (who, by the way, had not even invited Haman's wife Zeresh to the banquet) was certainly guilty! Achashveirosh could find a *better* queen (for example, Haman's own lovely daughter).

So Haman respectfully began:

"Your Majesty, I speak only for your good. Vashti has humiliated you publicly! What will people think? If a king cannot rule his own wife, how can he rule his empire? Oh, Your Majesty, do not end your fabulous banquet with this disgrace. Execute Vashti immediately! And, so that no one will follow her example, enact this new law: Any wife who won't listen to her husband will be killed!"

And so it was. The new law was decreed, and Vashti was burned at the stake that afternoon.

"Vaaa-jzz-teee! Vaaa-jzz-teee! Huhwherezz Vazjti?"

Achashveirosh grunted and rolled open his eyes. Dazzling yellow sunlight poured in through purple curtains. What was he doing in his private chamber — and what was he doing in bed?

"Huhwhere's my banquet? Huhwhere's everyone? HUHWHERE'S VASHTI?"

"Y-Your Majesty." The chief attendant approached him. "You ordered that Vashti be, uh, executed!"

"What orders?" roared Achashveirosh. "Bring her here!"

But the dreadful news was soon confirmed.

"Ahggh! Oh, no!" he cried. "I thought that was a dream! A dream? Why, it was a nightmare! Vashti executed? Ooooh! My dearly beloved, my beautiful Vashti! Vashti, Vashti, Vashti!"

For weeks Achashveirosh mourned and moaned. How lovely Vashti had been! He could think of nothing else, until one of his attendants finally suggested, "Marry again, Your Majesty! Invite all the beautiful (but obedient!) girls to Shushan, choose the one you like best, and you will know that your wife is the most beautiful in the world!"

Achashveirosh sighed. "Well, all right. Why not? Let 127 agents bring the most beautiful girls of my empire to Shushan!"

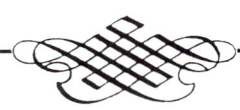

The Choice

Agents were soon on the lookout for beautiful girls in every province of the Persian empire.

Nishkanaz, the agent appointed to scout the district of Shushan, nervously chewed the tip of his clay stylus. "The most beautiful girl in Shushan," he murmured, "is hiding! Where will I find her? Especially today! Why, the streets of Shushan are mobbed with girls! I can hardly cross from one side to another — excuse me, excuse me! — with all of them trying to look so beautiful!"

Haman was standing on the side of the road with his daughter, who was attired in her most glittering robes and dazzling jewels. Anxiously, he peered up and down the crowded street until he finally spotted Nishkanaz making his way through the bustling throng.

"There, my dear!" whispered her father. "He's staring at you now! Go closer, so he can get a better look."

Haman shoved his daughter right under the nose of the Shushan agent, nearly tripping him.

"Ugghh!" Nishkanaz backed off. "I'm sick and tired of being pushed around by all these would-be queens — some of them have no manners at all! Why doesn't the *right* one make herself known?

"Where, oh, where," he continued to mumble, "is that mystery girl of Shushan?"

For days Nishkanaz searched. Along the wide, paved highways, through the lovely gardens and courtyards, up and down the narrow streets, and through every twisting alley, Nishkanaz looked. He called sweetly, "Beautiful girls, where *a-a-are* you?"

Sometimes he received no answer, and then he changed his tone. "Don't try to hide from the king's agent, or you will regret it!"

Finally, after many days . . .

"I've found her! Make way! Make way! Nishkanaz has found the girl whom the king will surely choose!"

Trumpets blared, horns blew, and the people of Shushan scurried to the side to make way. The king's horses were coming! Everyone could hear them prancing down the main highway. And who was in the royal carriage? Everyone pushed through the crowd to see.

"Is she really the one?"

"Don't you see? She is as lovely as they say!"

"More than lovely! She looks like beauty itself!"

"They say her name is Esther."

"Esther . . . Esther . . . my name is Esther!"

The contestant from Shushan repeated to herself, "I am to be called Esther! I am no longer Hadassah, the niece of Mordechai the Jew! My name is Esther, a Persian word for beautiful, but in Hebrew it means 'the hidden one.'"

For if they take you to the palace, you must hide that you are a Jew! Promise me that, Hadassah!

"Those were the last words that my dear uncle Mordechai spoke to me!" Esther thought as she sat alone on the silk cushions of the royal carriage. "If only I didn't have to leave the house this morning! If only I could have stayed with Mordechai, who has raised me from the cradle since my parents died. But to be queen to that drunken Achashveirosh!

"'*Ach, rosh!*' my people call him. The headache! But Mordechai warned me not to hide any longer. The king's agents said that anyone found hiding would be punished! I can't believe that Achashveirosh would ever think of choosing me for his queen. And yet, I won't forget what my uncle said."

If, nevertheless, you do become queen, it is the will of the Holy One, Blessed be He! Remember, Hadassah — you are now Esther! Should the king become angry at his queen, he might rage against her people. You must hide that you are a Jew!

A great bronze door, taller than any Esther had ever seen, swung open. Curious royal servants eyed her from all sides as Nishkanaz announced, "The contestant from Shushan!"

The royal silver trumpets blasted, and everyone bowed to her, including wizened old Hagai, the Chief Minister of the Contestants.

Hagai led her through the tall marble halls, corridor after royal corridor, until they came to a spacious chamber, where Hagai clapped his gnarled hands and ordered, "Refreshments for the contestant from Shushan!"

Immediately servants appeared, laden with heavy silver trays overflowing with delicacies. Golden roasted pheasant! Tangy, tantalizing turtle soup, pungent pickled peacock tongues, creamy honeyed cuckoo eggs, delectable marinated octopus stew. All from the king's own table — but nothing that was kosher!

"How generous of you to bring me this royal feast!" Esther said. "But honored master, I am not used to such a royal diet. If I find favor in your eyes, then let my meals be only raw fruits and vegetables, as I am accustomed to, and may the G-d of hospitality repay you for your kindness!"

"Gracious mistress, I am at your service!" Hagai bowed sincerely and Esther sighed in relief.

Platters of fruits and vegetables were brought in.

"She must be a vegetarian," whispered one of the serving girls.

"Is *that* her secret?" another replied. "I wondered how she appeared so regal." She added in a louder voice, "She is not yet queen, and already I hear she is going to have seven ladies-in-waiting!"

"Seven ladies-in-waiting?" thought Esther. "Then I can use a different servant for each day of the week, and none of them will ever notice that I act differently on Shabbos. With G-d's help, I will be able to keep all the mitzvos, and no one in the palace will know that I am a Jew!"

"Just look at her!" thought Hagai. "Not only is she elegant and charming, but her smile is kind and gentle. She radiates royalty! No doubt she will be the king's choice!"

"Did you hear? Did you hear? The king has chosen Esther! Esther is the new queen of Persia!"

From the throne room to the palace, through the courtyard and all of Shushan, all over the 127 provinces and across the entire world, the news spread. Trumpets roared and people cheered. The king had chosen a queen.

Esther, the beautiful Esther. But Esther of where? Mysterious Esther! No one knew where she came from, but everyone had something to say — everyone from the highest-ranking nobles to Shochadraz, the palace laundry maid.

"If you ask me," commented Shochadraz, "the king had his eye on her from the start!"

"He certainly did!" cried Habak, the dustmaid. "Did he even ask where she came from? He wouldn't have cared if she came from the moon! He *still* doesn't know! But he crowned her queen, and right away hung up her portrait in place of Vashti's!"

"Well, you know," said Lycia of the linen closets, "Esther was not your normal contestant. She never asked one thing for herself on the day she went to the king! She could have had rings for each finger, earrings to her shoulders, bracelets to her elbows, and necklaces to the floor. Why, there wasn't one other girl who didn't go to the king bedecked with ornaments from head to toe! But not Esther! I heard she wanted to wear a simple street dress, but Hagai wouldn't let her."

"I never saw anything like it!" Shochadraz added. "Esther was always busy taking care of other people. You know, when my son Farojollah had a sore throat, she gave me herbs to heal him!"

"Any contestant who was homesick always felt better after talking to her," added Habak. "Now the king himself asks her for advice. On her say-so, he appointed a new counselor — Mordechai the Jew!"

"Hmmmph!" sniffed Shochadraz. "Has Esther got connections with Jews?"

"Certainly not!" chuckled Habak. "Esther a friend of Mordechai's? Not after what he did to her! Why, when Esther refused to tell Achashveirosh what country she was from, Mordechai advised him to look for another queen! And do you know what? He did! Achashveirosh started his contest all over again, but in the end he still found no one he liked as much as Esther. So he simply stopped looking!"

And so did Mordechai. After two contests, Achashveirosh still wanted Esther. So, Mordechai reasoned, it must be the will of the Holy One, Blessed be He, that Esther be queen.

The Prime Minister

"Haaah!"

Haman, son of Hamedassa, of the family of Agag, from the infamous tribe of Amalek, threw back his shoulders and eloquently lifted his chin. He, the new prime minister, was now second in command to the king! In fact, a royal carpenter was just finishing Haman's new chair, which stood one head taller than those of the other advisors.

"And now," thought Haman, "I shall walk through the courtyard, and everyone will prostrate himself to the very ground as I walk by! And I shall wear my favorite idol around my neck." He gloated over the idea of everyone bowing down to the idol of Haman.

"But who is that?" Haman squinted as he stepped out into the bright Persian sunlight and gazed across the courtyard. Was there someone who was not bowing?

"*Ach!*" he fumed. "It is the Jew Mordechai who dares to stand! He will not bow to me because of this idol that I wear around my neck. He will bow only to his Jewish G-d! It boils my Amalekite blood. He not only insults me, but my god and my whole family too! But he'll be sorry. He will regret it.

"But why stop with Mordechai?" Haman rubbed his hands together with a pleasure he had not felt since becoming prime minister. "Yes, indeed — why stop with Mordechai? I will wipe out *all* the Jews — every last one!"

The Plot

The night was still. In the distant mountains, a lone hyena howled at the moon, which drifted through the hazy clouds. Everyone in Shushan slept, except for Bigsan and Teresh, who guarded the royal apartment.

"I've had it!" Angrily, Bigsan sat down on a stone, pulled off his boots, and rubbed his feet. "Teresh, it's too much! We used to be important advisors to the king, and now what's left for us? Guard duty! We don't even get to sleep nights anymore. My poor, aching feet! What a disgrace! Our dear cousin Vashti would never have let this happen!"

He sighed. "Yes, poor dear cousin Vashti. It's all Esther's fault. She gave our job to Mordechai! Hmmmph!" Then Bigsan grinned wickedly. "Perhaps we could give Esther's job to — well, someone else."

"Yeah!" Teresh nodded. "That would serve her right. But how would we do it?"

"The same way they gave Vashti's job to someone else!"

"Oh! You don't mean . . ."

"Yes!" Bigsan whispered, inching closer. "And with Esther out of the way, we can give Mordechai's job to someone else, and with Mordechai out of the way, we could even give Achashveirosh's job to someone else!"

"Oh, I get it!" said Teresh slowly. "Get rid of them and get someone else!" He sobered. "But Bigsan — the guards! The guards will see!"

"Of course they will, Teresh! But who are the guards?"

"Me. I'm a guard. And you — you're a guard."

"Right! Get it? *We* are the guards!"

"Yeah, I get it. But how are we going to guard them if we get rid of them?"

"Shhh!" hissed Bigsan. "Not so loud. Look, there's Mordechai, out for his early morning walk. It's a good thing we're speaking our own language. Anyway, Teresh, you just guard and be quiet, and I'll take care of the rest!"

"Don't worry, Bigsan!" said Teresh. "I will never tell anyone about Esther and Mordechai and Achashveirosh, and how we're going to get rid of them! Not me! Not a word!"

"Shhh!" Bigsan elbowed Teresh in the ribs as Mordechai passed by. "Shhh!"

Esther approached the king soon afterward to warn him of the planned assassination.

"But how did Mordechai know about it?" Achashveirosh questioned.

"Your Majesty," Esther replied, "Bigsan and Teresh did not realize that your servant Mordechai understands the Tarsian language. As a member of the Jewish Sanhedrin, he knows all the seventy languages of the world! He sent me at once to tell you of their dreadful plan."

"*Ach!* They would have poisoned me!" Achashveirosh bellowed. "Let everyone in Shushan see these rogues hanging from the gallows!"

And so it was. Bigsan and Teresh were hanged, and the entire incident was recorded in the royal chronicles. Esther took no credit for herself, and instead instructed the scribes to write that Mordechai had saved the king's life.

The Pur

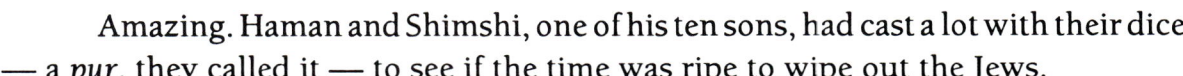

Amazing. Haman and Shimshi, one of his ten sons, had cast a lot with their dice — a *pur*, they called it — to see if the time was ripe to wipe out the Jews.

The dice, marked with Hebrew letters, landed on —

"*Alef, gimmel, gimmel!* What good fortune!" Haman clapped his hands. "That spells Agag, our family name. The dice show that Agag will come out on top!"

"On top of what?" Shimshi asked cautiously. "What are the letters underneath?"

Haman carefully overturned the dice. "*Dalet, vav, dalet!*" he cried. "That spells David! The Jews are called the people of David. Shimshi, it's clear as the sun — we are on top, and they are beneath us. We'll win! We'll finish them! We'll wipe them out at last!"

Haman cast another *pur* and picked the 13th of Adar as the date for the destruction of the Jewish people.

The Ring

Haman sauntered into the throne room, his sword gleaming brightly at his side. The guard hastily bowed and stepped back as Haman bustled directly to the king.

"Your Majesty," Haman began, "scattered throughout your provinces are a certain conceited people. They neither eat our food nor speak our language. They even refuse to marry with anyone besides their own (not that you should want to marry one of them, anyway — ha! ha!) — and they make trouble! They have their own holidays, while we good Persians are working hard to make a living. And day after day they dream that their G-d will rescue them and rebuild that Temple of theirs, which we worked so hard to destroy."

"Ah!" thought Achashveirosh. "He means the Jews. The Jews, whom my stargazers say will one day take over my throne!"

"Your Majesty would do well to be rid of these people!" said Haman.

"How right you are!" thought Achashveirosh. "But I am no fool! Their G-d will punish anyone who makes trouble for them!"

"And you don't have to be afraid of their G-d," said Haman, as though he could read Achashveirosh's thoughts. "Their G-d no longer cares for them. They themselves say that their G-d has abandoned them, like a master who has kicked his servant out of the house!

"Besides, it's so simple! Just decree that they should be — ahem — taken care of, and their enemies will take care of them. You won't have to do a thing! You have nothing to lose. I'll even pay you 10,000 loaves of silver! Just sign!"

"Well!" thought Achashveirosh. "The Jewish G-d can't blame *me* for taking care of a troublesome people! After all, that's my duty!"

He said aloud, "Very well, Haman. I appreciate your concern. The matter is in your hands. Here is my Ring of the Royal Seal!"

The ring! Haman's hands trembled as he clutched it. Now he had the power of the king. He could do whatever he pleased!

"Quickly!" hissed Haman to his sons as he gave them ink and papyrus scrolls. "These two decrees must go out tonight, before the king changes his mind! The first decree is for everyone in the empire. Read it, Shimshi!"

"Yes, Father." His son raised the scroll. "*Be ready for action on the 13th of Adar!* What action, Father?"

"The second decree, my sons, tells what the action is. But not everyone will receive *this* decree! Send it to the governors of the provinces only, as a secret message. Yes, the plan for the 13th of Adar must remain a secret! The Jews must not discover this action, or they might hide, flee, or even beg their G-d to save them. The action, my sons — our secret action — is to destroy the Jews!"

The Cry

The second decree did remain a secret . . . for four and a half minutes. Then Haman's stable boy happened to read it. He told no one, except the gardener. And the gardener told no one, except the cook. The cook told no one, except the porter, who spoke only to his friend — until cries were heard throughout all of Shushan.

"You Jew!"

"Me?" Reuven ben Shlomi, a Jew who lived in Shushan, could hardly believe that this accusation was coming from his fine Persian next-door neighbor, Shurshkuz.

"You Jew!" Shurshkuz growled again. "By the new declaration of Persia, you and your whole family will be killed, and I will take everything! Even those silver candlesticks that your wife likes so much will be mine!"

Reuven was too astonished to answer. But not his young son Yudi.

"That's what *you* think, Shurshkuz!" Yudi retorted. "Our G-d will protect us! We'll pray to Him, and you'll see! We won't be begging *you* for our lives. You'll be begging *us*!"

"You impertinent cockroach!" Shurshkuz leaped to give Yudi a kick the boy would never forget. Unfortunately for Shurshkuz, he stumbled over his own boots and fell flat on his nose.

"Euuuuuh!" groaned Shurshkuz, but his moans were dimmed by an even greater moan — the cry of all the Jews of Shushan, whose fate was now sealed.

Achashveirosh and Haman, however, heard nothing. They celebrated the decrees with full cups of merry wine and went to sleep with smiles on their faces.

Three Boys

With a hop and a skip, Haman left the palace. He would accomplish what other Amalekites had only dreamed of doing. He would kill all the Jews!

Meanwhile, Mordechai had also heard of the terrible decree. "What will happen now?" he wondered.

He glanced down the street. "Here are three young boys coming home from yeshiva. I will ask them what they learned in our holy Torah. That may help us decide what to do."

"Here is what we learned," replied the first boy. "My teacher told us not to be afraid of sudden terror!"

"And this is what *we* learned," exclaimed the second boy. "The wicked may have a plot, but their plans will fail — because G-d is with us!"

At once the third boy cried, "G-d made us! He'll take care of us! He'll help and rescue us!"

"So!" thought Mordechai. "Surely this is a sign that G-d will help us, no matter what Haman has planned!"

"What did those children say to you?" Haman's voice growled behind Mordechai's back.

Mordechai calmly turned around. "They say your plans will come to nothing!"

"I'll show them!" hissed Haman. "I'll take care of those children first. And you, Mordechai — you'll be next!"

The Fast

There was no time to lose. Achashveirosh had already signed Haman's terrible decree. Mordechai dressed in sackcloth, put ashes on his body, and went with a heavy heart toward the marketplace.

"My dear Jewish people!" he called through the streets of Shushan. "The king and Haman have announced their plan to kill us all! They have blocked the roads! We cannot escape! All the provinces know of the decree, and no place is safe for us! Only our G-d, the King of kings, can help us! If we cry out to Him, He will save us!"

"Listen!" exclaimed Reuven ben Shlomi. "Is that Mordechai?"

"It is!" replied Ben Begged the tailor. "And he's right! He has been right all along. Instead of longing to return to the Holy Land of Israel, we have been busy going to parties with the Persians!"

"And we have bargained at bazaars instead of studying G-d's laws," Reuven admitted. "Will G-d forgive us?"

"Does G-d even remember who we are?" exclaimed Ben Begged.

"Yes! Mordechai is telling us that our G-d still cares about us and will save us!"

Soon all the Jews of Shushan were crying to the King of kings, begging Him to forgive them and to deliver them from danger. Yes, all the Jews were crying to the Merciful One — except a few.

"Not me!" insisted Devar ben Rik. "I'm not going to cry like a baby! Isn't Mordechai the king's advisor? And isn't Esther the queen? We know that she's a Jew. We don't have to worry. Esther will take care of us!"

"But how can I?" Esther wrote to Mordechai. "The king has not sent for me for thirty days. And to go to the king uninvited — why, that means death, unless he holds out his golden scepter!"

"Don't wait!" urged Mordechai by return message. "Already Jews are being attacked in the far-off provinces! This may be the very reason you were chosen to be queen. Tell the king now that you are a Jew, and save your people!"

"I am not afraid!" Esther replied. "I ask only that you gather all the Jews of Shushan, and fast and pray for me for three days and three nights. My servant girls and I will also fast. And then, although it is against the law, I will go to the king and plead for my people. If I die, I die!"

That night was Pesach, the night of the first *seder*. But the Jews of Persia fasted. "Better to fast on one *seder* so that we may live to keep many," Mordechai decreed as he gathered all the Jews of Shushan, including 12,000 *kohanim*. Each *kohen* took a *shofar* in his right hand and a Torah scroll in his left.

"L-rd of the Universe!" cried the *kohanim*. "You gave Your Torah to us! If we, Your people, are all killed, who will be left to study Your Torah? Who will keep its mitzvos? Please answer us! Do not let Your people be destroyed!"

Then the *kohanim* blew their *shofaros* . . .

A great blast burst through the air, growing louder and louder, blowing the tears and prayers of all the Jews of Shushan straight through the very heavens.

The Request

Rukisa, the second of Esther's servant girls, squirmed. The sackcloth felt rough, the ashes were grimy, and she had been wearing them now for almost three days. And for three days she had seen Esther lying face down on the floor, crying to the One Above for mercy. Of course, Rukisa and Esther's other servant girls were crying for mercy too.

Yes, the decree had also affected them. Esther was not only their kind and gentle queen. She was also their wise teacher, for Rukisa and her six friends had all secretly decided to become Jews. If the decree were not overturned, they would die as well!

Suddenly, before the third day of the fast was over, Esther arose, bathed, and dressed in her most elegant silk gown. She adorned herself with her most precious gems, and even wore the special crown that Achashveirosh had given her when she became queen. How calm Esther looked, and how regal!

"Chulsa! N'hursa! Rukisa!" Esther summoned three of her maids. "Please dress quickly in your most courtly gowns, and accompany me to the king!"

To the king? To the king's very throne room? But Achashveirosh had not called for Esther! By the law of the land, no one was allowed to go to the king without an invitation. And look what had happened to Vashti when *she* disobeyed him! She was killed for not coming when he called her. Achashveirosh could very well do the same to Esther for coming when he *didn't* call her!

"My queen will give up her life to save her people!" thought Rukisa. "And I will follow her!"

Esther had never looked so beautiful as she and her three maidens slowly and majestically left the queen's quarters. Only Rukisa, who held the queen's hand, felt Esther's pulse race as they approached the inner court hall and the seven chambers guarded by seven platoons of guards.

Would the guards stop the queen? Esther did not hesitate, but calmly stepped closer and closer toward the guards, whose jeweled swords shimmered in the sunlight.

The head guard of the first platoon eyed her. He had not been told to admit the queen. He would stop her!

But no. The queen was coming in all her glory. And her face — it shone with awesome power! Hastily the head guard stepped back and bowed respectfully, while Esther and her maidens continued to the second chamber. Here again the guards did not stop them, but only stepped back in awe.

And so Esther entered the third chamber, the fourth, the fifth, the sixth — and the seventh.

But suddenly she trembled. She had reached the innermost courtyard, and found herself surrounded by idols on all sides! She felt overwhelmed and grew faint. Her maidens supported her until the queen had passed the idols, and once again Esther looked royal and composed, even as she approached the throne room.

When the king saw her standing in the doorway, he grew speechless with rage. How dare Esther break the law! How dare she come uncalled!

His guards clutched their spears and unsheathed their swords, greedily eyeing Esther's jewelry and the precious stones on her gown. They could grab these for themselves, if the king would only give the word!

They watched as the king rose to his feet, his eyes flashing with fury, his fingers white as they gripped the arm of his throne.

And suddenly, as though someone had slapped him across the face to bring him to his senses, his anger left him. Achashveirosh lowered his golden scepter.

"My beautiful queen!" he exclaimed. "Why are you so pale? Certainly the law that forbids anyone to come to the throne room without an invitation does not apply to *you*! You are my dear queen! Tell me now — what do you desire? Ask even for half my kingdom — and it shall be yours!"

Rukisa felt the queen's hand tremble. Yes, he had extended to Esther the golden scepter, but now was not the time to ask for more favors.

"If it pleases the king," Esther began, "let the king and Haman come to a feast that I have prepared for them!"

"Haman too?" asked Achashveirosh.

"Yes," Esther replied. "I have been very ungrateful to Haman. If it were not for his advice concerning Vashti, I would never have become queen! Let him also come!"

"Hmmmph," snorted Achashveirosh. "Well, all right. In the name of Queen Esther, summon Haman to the feast!"

The Gallows

Haman was delighted. What a wonderful banquet — a dream come true! He, Haman, the son of Hamedassa, had just dined at a private feast with the king and the queen! He could hardly wait to tell his wife and friends. Oh, how elegant it had been — how superb, how exclusive!

And he had been invited by the queen herself. He, Haman, was not only prime minister of Persia, but he was also a favorite of the queen! She had served him such an excellent meal, as though she wanted to show how much she admired him. And then, after a delectable dessert and an abundance of wine, the king had said to Esther:

"My dear queen! Tell me! What is it your heart desires? I will give it to you — even if it is half my kingdom!"

And the queen? What had she replied? Haman could hardly believe his ears when she said, "Please, if it finds favor in the king's eyes, then let the king — and Haman — come to another party that I shall make for them tomorrow."

Another party! Haman hardly felt the ground beneath his feet as he, the most honored, respected, privileged man in the world, left the palace, with everyone bowing to him. They bowed on his left, they bowed on his right, until he came to the king's gate and saw . . .

"That Mordechai! Standing again!" Haman later exploded to his wife Zeresh and to his friends. "In spite of all my power, in spite of all my wealth, *and* my invitations from the queen! In spite of everything, Mordechai insults me every day!"

"Well, *do* something about it!" Zeresh exclaimed. "You could build a gallows for that Mordechai right here on our front yard! Build it fifty cubits high so that you can see it from the palace. Then, tomorrow morning when Mordechai is praying, simply go to the king and mention that Mordechai deserves to be hanged for not believing in the Persian gods. Certainly the king will do you that little favor! And afterwards, when you are dining with the king and queen, you will have even greater pleasure as you gaze out the window — and watch Mordechai hang!"

"Yes, yes!" Haman agreed. "Let the gallows be built immediately."

"I will call my friends, and we will make a party of it!" said Zeresh.

And so she did. Zeresh and her friends played music while Haman and his sons sang and hammered late into the night.

"Finished!" Haman exclaimed at last. "Now, let me just make sure that it's the right height!"

He climbed to the top of the scaffold and, for a joke, tied the rope around his own neck. "Look, everyone!" He was grinning. "A perfect fit!"

The Sleepless Night

Now that the gallows was finished, Haman was too excited to sleep.

"I'll just stroll down to the Jewish Quarter," he thought, "to have one last look at Mordechai!"

But the streets of the Jewish Quarter were more calm than Haman had expected.

"I hear the voices of small children," he muttered. "Why do their mothers let them stay up so late? There they are! Hundreds of them, all gathered around that old man dressed in sackcloth — why, it's Mordechai! Why would a doomed man like Mordechai spend his last minutes teaching Torah to little children?"

"Throw those children in prison!" Haman commanded to his private police.

But in jail it was just as bad. The children continued to babble their annoying prayers. And to make matters worse, all their mothers came running with food, urging their children to eat before they died!

"The nerve of those children!" fumed Haman. "They don't even listen to their mothers. Every last one of them is placing his school book over his heart and insisting that he would rather die fasting! Even here in the dungeon they are praying to their Jewish G-d, until the whole foundation of my prison is shaking!"

And the children's prayers did go straight to heaven. The Merciful One heard them and decreed that the Jews should live. The Al-mighty then awoke the only person in Shushan who had gone to bed peacefully that night — King Achashveirosh.

Achashveirosh tossed and turned. As exhausted as he was after feasting with Esther and Haman, he could not fall asleep; every time he closed his eyes, voices seemed to awaken him.

"Ungrateful one!" they exclaimed. "Reward those who have helped you!"

"What? Me? Ungrateful?" Achashveirosh groggily tried to remember. "When? To whom? For what? I don't recall a thing! Scribe! Bring the Book of the Royal Records!"

The scribe Shimshi, son of Haman, brought the thick heavy book of the royal chronicles. When he opened it, he saw the account of the plot of Bigsan and Teresh.

"Better read something else!" thought Shimshi, but when he tried to turn to another page, the wind blew it right back. Again he turned the page, but again it blew back.

"Fool!" screamed the king. "Read!"

"Uh . . . uh . . ."

While Shimshi stood stammering, the page began to read itself! *Mordechai the Jew saved the king's life!*

"Why, so he did." Achashveirosh smiled. "Loyal Mordechai! I remember it well. What reward did he receive?"

"Uh, mmm, none, Your Majesty," replied Shimshi.

"None? Well, then! I will reward him first thing in the morning!"

His mind now at ease, Achashveirosh fell asleep. But his dreams were not pleasant. He saw before him Haman, as large as life, grasping a brilliant sword and preparing to kill both the king and the queen!

A sudden banging at the door startled Achashveirosh.

"Who — who is that?" the king demanded. And standing there before his very bed was — Haman!

"Haman?" Achashveirosh quickly rubbed the sleep from his eyes. Haman had never come so early before; in fact, he was always the last to arrive at the palace. "Perhaps he *does* want to kill me!" thought Achashveirosh. "He might even want to be king himself! I'm going to test him."

"Haman," demanded the king, "I have a question to ask you, a most important question. What shall be done to the man whom the king wishes to honor?"

"*Honor!*" thought Haman. "Well! Whom would the king want to honor more than me?"

"Your Majesty," he began, "let this man be dressed in royal robes! Let him be escorted by the king's most royal servant! Let him be led on the royal horse through the main street of Shushan, and let the servant proclaim, 'So shall be done to the man whom the king wishes to honor!' "

Haman lowered his eyes modestly, waiting to receive his honor.

"Haman," commanded Achashveirosh, "do all that you have said — to Mordechai!"

"Oooooh-wooohh!" Haman moaned.

He had to climb up to the Royal Wardrobe, where the king's coronation robe was stored. Then he had to go to the royal stables to prepare Shifragaz, the king's best horse. And as though that were not enough, he now had to go out and search for Mordechai.

"Mordechai!" Haman had to force the humiliating words from his throat. "Arise! By orders of the king, I must dress you!"

"Have you no respect for the king?" exclaimed Mordechai. "I have been wearing sackcloth and ashes for three days! For the honor of His Majesty, I must bathe first and have a haircut."

"Bathe? Haircut?" sputtered Haman. "But there is no bathhouse or barber shop open in all of Shushan. They are all closed in honor of the procession in which *you* are going to ride!"

He moaned, "I have no choice. I must attend to Mordechai myself. So important a man as I — reduced to barber and bath attendant!"

A few hours later . . .

"All right, Mordechai. It is done! Now mount the horse!"

"I am too weak," Mordechai replied. "I have been fasting for three days!"

"Then I'll bow down, and you can step on my back!" cried Haman in despair.

"Good!" thought Mordechai. "It is as our sages tell us: We shall step on the backs of our enemies."

And so the procession began.

"Look!" Young Yudi ben Reuven pointed from his window. "Here come a thousand men, all carrying golden cups on satin pillows! They're marching in front of Mordechai! Listen to them shout!"

So shall be done to the man whom the king wishes to honor!

"Why, this is marvelous!" exclaimed Haman's daughter as she watched the parade from her window. "Mordechai is about to be hanged, and he is now leading my father on the horse! That Mordechai, who wouldn't even bow down to my father! Well, I'll show him!" And with a snicker of delight, she threw a pot of garbage onto Mordechai's head.

But no . . . the man who looked up at her with filth dripping down his face was not Mordechai. It was—

Her father! She had thrown filth over her own father!

"Ooooohhh!" Haman's daughter swooned, fainted, and fell out the window, as the parade marched on.

The Second Banquet

Haman wished he could disappear. The parade was over. No one wanted to be near him. They turned away from him as if he were garbage — well, he *was* covered with garbage. It oozed all over his robes and down his neck. And his own daughter had thrown it on him — his own beautiful daughter, whom he had wanted to be queen!

"But I will still hang Mordechai!" Haman vowed as he stood in his own parlor afterward, wiping off his face.

His wife, who was the most expert stargazer in Persia, was not so sure. "Mordechai is a Jew," she said. "The Jews are not like other people. Today they may seem as low as the dust of the earth, but tomorrow their G-d may save them, and they will become as high as the stars."

Just then the Persian chief of police barged in. "How dare you keep the king and queen waiting!" he growled; and before Haman even had time to change his clothing, he was whisked off to Esther's second banquet.

Esther had prepared everything, including plenty of wine to soothe her guests after the eventful day. Achashveirosh relaxed as he drained his cup. Once more he turned to Esther and asked, "What is your wish, my dear queen? Ask whatever you desire! Ask even for half my kingdom, and it shall be yours!" With a sigh he poured a second cup and awaited a reply.

Esther rose. "If I have pleased the king," she began, "and if the king thinks it is good, then my wish is . . . that the king give me my life, and also the lives of my people!"

"What?" Achashveirosh gasped, nearly spilling his cup.

"Yes!" Esther continued. "An order has been decreed that all the Jewish people be killed. And *I am a Jew!* I am a descendant of the famed King Shaul, of the tribe of Binyamin!"

"Who? Which? What?" Achashveirosh stammered, vaguely remembering some talk of killing the Jews. "Who would dare do it?"

"A terrible man — an enemy! This evil Haman!" Esther pointed, Haman trembled, and Achashveirosh was so upset that he ran out to the palace garden.

Suddenly it all became clear to the king. If Esther was a Jew, then her children would be Jewish. So *his* children would be Jewish! The stargazers were right. A Jew — his own son — would someday sit on the throne!

Incredible! Esther, who was his wife, was a Jew. Mordechai, who had saved his life, was a Jew. And Haman, who had advised Achashveirosh to kill Vashti... was now in the palace with Esther.

"Why, Haman might want to kill Esther too!" Achashveirosh exclaimed. He dashed back to the palace, yanked open the door, and...

"Yyyuuuuw!" The sudden creaking of the enormous doors startled Haman so much that he toppled over Esther.

"Do you dare to attack the queen?" raged Achashveirosh. "Guards! Arrest this villain!"

"Look, Your Majesty!" exclaimed Charvonah, an advisor who happened to be standing nearby. "See there! Those are the gallows that Haman prepared last night for the loyal Mordechai, who spoke on behalf of the king!"

"Excellent! Hang Haman on the very gallows that he built for Mordechai!"

At the king's word, the palace guards covered Haman's head with the hangman's hood. He would never see the face of the king again.

Purim

"Esther — look over there!"

Achashveirosh waved his hand toward the palace window. "There swings Haman, on gallows fifty cubits high! Everyone in Shushan can see that I have fulfilled your request. Yet, you still look worried!"

"Your Majesty," Esther pleaded, "Haman himself is hanging, but his decree lives on. His proclamation has reached the farthest provinces of Persia. Please, please, rescind his proclamation!"

"Alas," sighed Achashveirosh. "That I cannot do! By the law of Persia, a decree stamped with the king's royal seal can never be revoked. And yet... perhaps there *is* a way. Yes! I should have thought of it before!

"Haman is a criminal, and by the law of Persia, the decree of a criminal is worthless. We must only let it be known that Haman has been hanged! Then we will proclaim that Mordechai is my new prime minister. Now, if anyone dares to attack the Jews — the Jews have my royal permission to fight back! So I decree!"

"Did you hear the new decree?" exclaimed Ben Begged to Reuven ben Shlomi. "It's a miracle! G-d has heard our prayers and will save us!"

"It is a miracle!" cried Mordechai to Esther. "Every Jew in Persia is so happy that they are resolving all over again to keep the entire Torah!"

And everyone rejoiced. The courtyards were spread with myrtle branches and bedecked with purple curtains. Young boys carrying small crowns danced in the streets. The *kohanim* blew trumpets, and Haman's ten sons were paraded in chains before Mordechai. Even the Persians were awed by Mordechai the Jew, who wore his *tallis* and *tzitzis* over his royal robes and his *tefillin* in front of his crown.

And when the 13th of Adar came, no one dared to support the enemies of the Jews. Outside of Shushan, the Jews defeated their foes in an overwhelming victory in only one day. In Shushan itself the forces of Amalek were stronger, and the fighting continued one day longer, until the enemies of the Jews were completely vanquished.

And when the fighting was over on the 14th of Adar (and in Shushan, on the 15th), a grand celebration took place! Everyone feasted, everyone drank. Soldiers returning from battle gave gifts to their friends, and everyone gave gifts to the poor, so that they could celebrate as well.

"This should be a holiday for Jews for all times!" cried Esther as she gave Mordechai an account she had written of the wondrous events. When the Sanhedrin read it, they realized that she had composed it with *ruach hakodesh*, divine inspiration, and they included it with the other holy writings of the Jewish people.

"What should they call this new holiday?" Mordechai asked.

"Purim," Esther replied, "after the lottery — the *pur* of Haman."

Mordechai nodded as he looked at Esther's young son, Daryavesh. Daryavesh would soon be crowned king of Persia, at only six years of age. Then, with wisdom beyond his years, he would order the Holy Temple to be rebuilt in Jerusalem.

There would still be hard times for the Jewish people. But every year, Esther's *megillah* and the story of Purim would remind all Jews that even at times when G-d seems very far away, He is really very close . . .

Until finally a new time will come, very soon. Then the Third Great Temple will be built, never to be destroyed —

And all the Jewish people will rejoice forever, as on the holiday of Purim!